LOVE YOUR JOB

Based on *WorkJoy* by Beth Stallwood

First published in Great Britain by Practical Inspiration Publishing, 2026

© Beth Stallwood and Practical Inspiration Publishing, 2026

The moral rights of the author have been asserted

ISBN 978-1-78860-898-5 (paperback)
978-1-78860-899-2 (ebook)

All rights reserved. This book, or any portion thereof, may not be reproduced without the express written permission of the publisher.

Every effort has been made to trace copyright holders and to obtain their permission for the use of copyright material. The publisher apologizes for any errors or omissions and would be grateful if notified of any corrections that should be incorporated in future reprints or editions of this book.

EU GPSR representative: LOGOS EUROPE, 9 rue Nicolas Poussin, LA ROCHELLE 17000, France Contact@logoseurope.eu.

Want to bulk-buy copies of this book for your team and colleagues? We can customize the content and co-brand *Love Your Job* to suit your business's needs.

Please email info@practicalinspiration.com for more details.

Contents

Series introduction

Welcome to *6-Minute Smarts*!

This is a series of very short books with one simple purpose: to introduce you to ideas that can make life and work better, and to give you time and space to think about how those ideas might apply to *your* life and work.

Each book introduces you to ten powerful ideas, but ideas on their own are useless – that's why each idea is followed by self-coaching questions to help you work out the 'so what?' for you in just six minutes of exploratory writing. What's exploratory writing? It's the kind of writing you do just for yourself, fast and free, without worrying what anyone else thinks. It's not just about getting ideas out of your head and onto paper where you can see them; it's about finding new connections and insights as you write. This is where the magic happens.

Whatever you're facing, there's a *6-Minute Smarts* book just for you. And once you've learned how to coach yourself through a new idea, you'll be smarter for life.

Find out more...

Introduction

I sat in the living room, staring out of the window. I'd been up since the early hours of the morning, too excited to sleep. Then there it was – a white Mercedes pulling into the driveway. It was 1990 and this was a very fancy car, with a driver, coming to take me to my first ever paid job (at the tender age of 8). I'd been given special permission to be off school and I was ready to burst. My mum and I jumped in, and we headed off to Pinewood Studios.

I toured the sound stages and water tanks where some of the greatest movies had been shot. Then I was ushered to my dressing room where the new outfit that the costume designer and I had chosen a few weeks before awaited me (including a pair of red Converse high tops – the height of fashion!). I got changed, they did my hair and make-up, and I headed to our set to spend two days filming with three grown-up actors.

After that, my first ever paid gig was complete and I headed home, back to school and back to normal life.

Up at the crack of dawn one Saturday morning months later, I wandered downstairs and turned on the TV. Hearing a loud scream, my parents ran downstairs to find out what was wrong. It was all over: I had just watched myself on TV for the first time. Multiple auditions, rehearsals and two days of filming condensed into one very short commercial for Heinz Tomato Ketchup. Luckily, my parents didn't have to wait long to see it for themselves – it was on a lot in the early 1990s.

I later discovered this is not a typical introduction to work. Chauffeur-driven cars, a year's supply of red sauce and being allowed to keep the outfit? Not the norm. Yet it sparked in me a love for working that's never stopped – even though I've done much less glamorous work since.

When I was in my teens, I dreamt big and was supported by parents who told me I could do anything I set my mind to. There was always one thing at the core, though. Once, when I was about 15, I was asked: 'What do you want to be when you grow up?' I thought for a moment and replied with one word: *Happy*. I didn't realize it then, but I'd stated my intent to focus on joy.

From being a barmaid to fitting kids' shoes, my early career is not so different from many others. I enjoyed having purpose beyond lectures, reading, rehearsing and writing essays while I was studying. Once I'd graduated, I got a temp job until I worked out what to do. From that, an unexpected career formed. I found myself training, coaching and leading teams in financial services. I moved to the public sector for a couple of years, and my last employed job was as a head of talent and development in the world of sport. Throughout, it's always been about people and enabling them to perform at their best.

Now I work independently as a consultant, speaker, coach and facilitator across industries and organizations of all different sizes and in different sectors. Through every role, every step-up and every organization I've worked with, I've been able to create and cultivate joy. Even when times have been tough, when hurdles were in the way, and when I couldn't quite see the light at the end of the tunnel, I found the route through. I can honestly say I have loved every single job I have ever done. None of them have been perfect. They have all been wonderful in their own way.

Working with such a diverse range of organizations and thousands of people has given me deep insight into what brings people joy at work, and the things that have the opposite effect. I've worked with organizations to create environments that encourage a better working life. I've coached leaders to enable them to engage and support their people in a positive way. I've supported individuals to take control of their working life, crafting careers that give them what they want and need.

This book is for you if you're ready to take personal responsibility for loving your job, whether you've recently fallen out of love with it or you're actively disliking it right now.

Let's spark the joy!

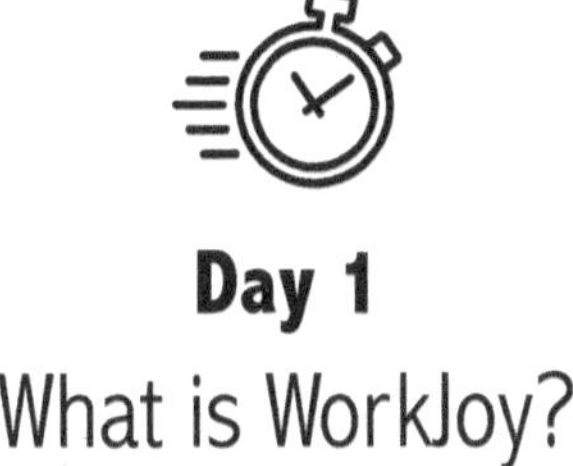

Day 1
What is WorkJoy?

The word that I use for that feeling of loving your job is WorkJoy. But what is it?

WorkJoy (noun): the positive, warm or happy feeling you get about your work, when working or at your workplace.

But a noun feels a little too passive. WorkJoy needs to be active, so let's make it a verb:

WorkJoy (verb): to develop the mindset and take action in pursuit of a better working life.

WorkJoy is something you feel on the inside that shows on the outside too. That warm feeling translates to a real smile, a positive tone in your voice and a little skip in your step. It stems from a hopeful place where you feel positive and energized. It builds your courage and makes you feel able to take on work-related challenges.

Sources of WorkJoy

Sources are varied and personal, ranging from micro to massive in impact:

Micro-moments	These are the little moments that really add up. Ticking off an item on a to-do list, a colleague saying hello or starting a fresh notepad. These fleeting moments of joy are just as important as the big things. They are also a great place to start when building your approach; they are easy to introduce and build great momentum.
Personal preferences	These are dependent on your style in any situation. You might feel joy from presenting to your team, or that might fill you with utter dread. Perhaps you attend some meetings that are inspiring, yet others leave you wanting to sit in a darkened room. There are likely some people at work that light you up and others that suck the positivity out of you. It is not the situation but the combination of factors that define whether it's a joyful experience for you.

Fundamental factors	These are the big things like purpose, leadership and organizational culture, the 'way things are done around here'. If, for example, there is a mismatch between your organization's culture and your preferences you may be facing an uphill battle to find joy.

Sources of WorkJoy are plentiful and tend to multiply. The combination that brings you consistent joy will be unique to you. Copying someone else's approach may inspire you but may not hit the mark for your style and circumstances.

The things that bring you WorkJoy may also change over time. Different roles bring different opportunities, changing life stages may require you to re-prioritize, and organizations will present you with a variety of challenges. Being prepared to flex and adapt is how you build a sustainable approach.

Defining WorkGloom

WorkGloom (noun): the negative, sad or frustrated feeling you get about your work, when working or at your workplace.

But WorkGloom isn't something you can simply pass off as something forced upon you. Apportioning blame without taking personal responsibility is a passive way of dealing with the gloom. Let's action this up instead and make it into a verb!

WorkGloom (verb): to adopt and embed the unhelpful habits that lead you into a downward spiral of work-based negativity that spills over into your life beyond work.

WorkGloom stifles energy and passion for work. Mild gloom feels a bit 'meh'; chronic gloom is crushing. It shows in a moany tone, a resting gloom face and even your posture.

Sources range from trivial yet impactful (someone not smiling at you) to bigger issues like leadership and communication. Some you create yourself; others happen to you. Your quest is to learn strategies, techniques and habits to tame and manage it.

But first, a couple of important points...

What WorkJoy *isn't* about

Taking responsibility for your WorkJoy is one thing, but this is *not* about passively accepting a toxic work environment, believing that everything that isn't right is somehow your fault, or continuing to be treated poorly in your workplace. If you're ever feeling bullied, harassed or unsafe, if you're experiencing discrimination or if there are unchallenged inappropriate behaviours happening in your organization, that's not OK and embarking on a WorkJoy quest won't fix things.

These factors go beyond the usual workplace annoyances and frustrations; they describe an unhealthy workplace culture. If you're stuck in a situation like this, please talk to someone you trust. Before you can learn to love your job, you'll need to address these issues or find somewhere different to work where you and your individual brilliance are valued.

A note on mental health

Mental health is at the heart of being able to embark on, and benefit from, your personal WorkJoy journey. If you're experiencing any mental health issues or feel that your levels of gloom have moved beyond the standard challenges that we all experience from time to time, please consult a mental health professional. This book isn't intended as a solution or treatment to mental health issues or mental illness.

Understanding WorkJoy over time

It can help to visualize what WorkJoy might look like in the real world over a period. This diagram shows an example of an average working week plotted with WorkJoy and WorkGloom moments, plus a central area entitled the *neutral zone*. Not everything that happens in a day will fit at the elation or misery end of the spectrum. For much of the time, you're likely to be betwixt the two!

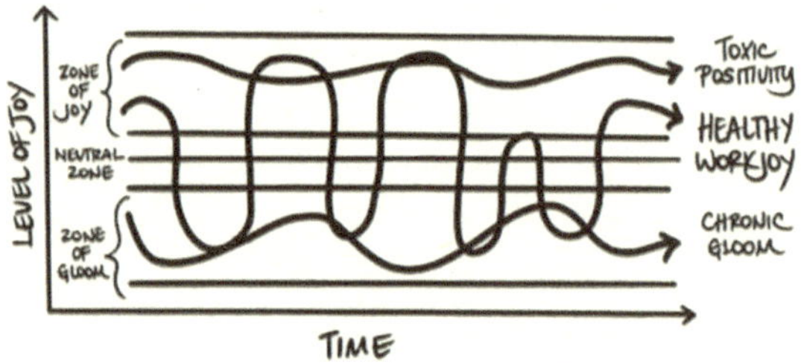

- **Healthy WorkJoy.** Joy and gloom ebb and flow. There's quick recovery from gloom, built through a practice of reframing and bolstered by solid levels of the good stuff. The joy sticks around for longer, built through a practice of noticing it and enhanced by reflecting on it.
- **Chronic WorkGloom.** Here the effects of a gloomy mindset, environment or situation

are evident. The neutral has a hint of gloom and tends to be below the line. Where there are moments of joy, they are low-level and short-lived. They give way to longer, deeper periods of gloom.

- **Toxic positivity.** On the surface this looks fantastic, right? But all lives have gloomy parts and denying that can send you into the zone of faking it – outwardly and, even more dangerously, convincing yourself that everything is wonderful!

Developing your WorkJoy mindset

Mindset is the way you think and the beliefs that help you navigate situations. The shift from 'meh' to 'yeah' starts in your head. It's an expedition you lead yourself on, but as you'll see you won't embark on it alone.

This adventure to fall in love with your job isn't a one-hit wonder. The magic sits in how you process your thoughts, develop your behaviours and create helpful habits. It's learning to focus your attention on the things that will make a difference, rather than getting stuck in the quagmire. Over time, this will lead you to better understand how to get more

WorkJoy, more often, as well as a deep understanding of how to reframe and manage the WorkGloom.

Where are you at right now?

A recent survey found 90% expected a substantial degree of joy at work, but only 37% actually experienced it – a 'joy gap' of 53%.[1] Let's take inspiration from this research and work out what your personal joy gap is.

Rate the level of joy you currently experience in an average week from 1–10 (1 = consistently gloomy and 10 = consistently joyful).

Now subtract your reality from a 10 (for the purposes of this exercise, a healthy and realistic level of WorkJoy!).

- Large joy gap (7+): you need a big dose of WorkJoy ASAP! You'll need to dig deep to make a significant change.
- Medium joy gap (4–6): consider which areas are worth focusing your attention on and get experimenting.
- Small joy gap (3 or less): brilliant – use this book to fine tune, supercharge, and maintain the joy.

Wherever you're at right now, the first tool for finding more joy is the three Es – Engagement, Energy and Experimentation – and that's where we'll start tomorrow.

So what? Over to you…

1. What's the shape of your WorkJoy right now – and how do you know?

2. Where are the sources of WorkJoy for you?

3. And what tends to bring about WorkGloom?

Day 2

Engage, energize, experiment

In Day 2 we're going to focus on the three Es of WorkJoy – Engagement, Energy and Experimentation – as approaches to creating and cultivating more love for your job.

Engagement

It's easy to drift into becoming a passive participant. Maybe you've found yourself stepping back or checking out at work? Have you stopped putting your hand up for new projects, asking for feedback or speaking in meetings? Perhaps you've heard yourself moaning yet not taking action to fix the issues you are facing? You can step into a more joyful mindset by paying attention to what's going on, engaging with your attitude and emotions about work.

Energy

Awareness is just the first step. You need not only to understand where you get your joy and gloom from, but also to dedicate yourself to action.

It's going to take effort and energy to improve your working life – that's a fact. You're busy – you've got more things on your to-do list than hours in the day to get them done. This is where choice comes into the frame.

You can carry on as you are, or you can choose to put some energy into making it better. You can choose to see this as more things on the to-do list, or you can see it as an investment into a brighter future. You can choose to embark on your quest for more joy, or you can choose not to take that step. Energy is the biggest catalyst for change.

Experimentation

Experimentation is the key that unlocks the door to loving your job. Just as the factors that create WorkJoy and WorkGloom are unique to you, so are the solutions to the conundrums you face. There are almost unlimited ways to explore what works for you.

To get into experimenting, be prepared to try new and different things, to break out of old habits and create new ones. Perhaps you may return to some things you've done before that have fallen off your agenda? Maybe you'll head down some avenues that aren't right for you, that's useful feedback too.

Be ready for it to feel awkward. When that feeling comes, don't step back or try to circumnavigate it. Walk directly into it, embrace it. That feeling happens just before growth, in the moments before you learn what you really need. Learn to embrace it and one day you may even love it!

Utilizing the three Es

You might find one E comes naturally – perhaps you're an engager, an energy-investor or an action-seeker. Others may feel harder. But you'll need to engage all three Es at some point during your quest for more WorkJoy, so it's important both to recognize your areas of strength and work through those areas that feel more daunting.

The WorkJoy formulae

How will the three Es help you love your job more? Essentially, there are two formulae you can use: a passive one and a more active one. Let's look at each in turn.

Passive WorkJoy formula

WorkJoy = WorkJoy moments – WorkGloom moments

The passive WorkJoy formula is the balance of the joyful moments in your life vs the gloomy moments in any given period, taking account of both the volume and the vigour of each moment:

- **Volume** is the number of times something happens and the regularity
- **Vigour** is the size and impact of the moment.

When something tiny happens regularly, it can bring you brilliant amounts of WorkJoy or land you in the pit of WorkGloom. This formula can also mean that one big thing, even if it only happens once, can have the same captivating or crushing impact.

In this passive formula, if you can reduce the gloom and build the joy moments, you will likely feel more WorkJoy. It's a good place to begin to better understand your sources of WorkJoy and WorkGloom.

Active WorkJoy formula

Once you understand where you get your WorkJoy and WorkGloom from, try this active formula to create greater impact through the choices you make and the actions you take. It focuses on utilizing the Engagement, Energy and Experimentation approach and applying it with intent in two different directions:

WorkJoy = (EEE x cultivating WorkJoy) + (EEE x reframing WorkGloom)

This formula can transform the way you think, feel and act at work (and beyond!).

Remember, you can never eliminate all the gloom. Focus your energy on the positive side of this formula and you'll find that the gloom seems to reduce in impact as you align to a joyful mindset.

With your three Es in hand, you have a practical framework to move from recognition to transformation. Next, we'll explore how your life beyond work interacts with WorkJoy – and how to make the balance serve you.

So what? Over to you…

1. Which of the three Es are you drawn to?

2. Which of them do you feel less connected to?

3. How might you focus on cultivating one E this week?

Day 3

Reclaim your work/life blend

Before we go any further, we're going to talk about life outside of work. Let's start by busting a very big, very annoying myth...

The myth of work/life balance

The very idea of 'work/life balance' carries lots of assumptions. For example:

- It puts work first. Work is an important part of life, but is it really the most important part?
- It implies you're not alive when you're working! There's so much life to be had at work – just think of the experiences, friends and sense of purpose it gives you.

- It assumes things stay static – but there are times when this simply isn't true. Sometimes life outside work takes over (building a family, moving house, caring, etc), sometimes work dominates (a big project, working towards a qualification or promotion, etc).

Trying to find a constant 'balance' is impossible, so you feel you've failed, and the self-pity party really gets going. How about we create a more realistic version of what work looks like in the context of life?

The balloons of life

Picture a large transparent balloon representing your whole life, with smaller balloons inside representing its key elements – friends, family, work (paid), unpaid work, hobbies, and so on.

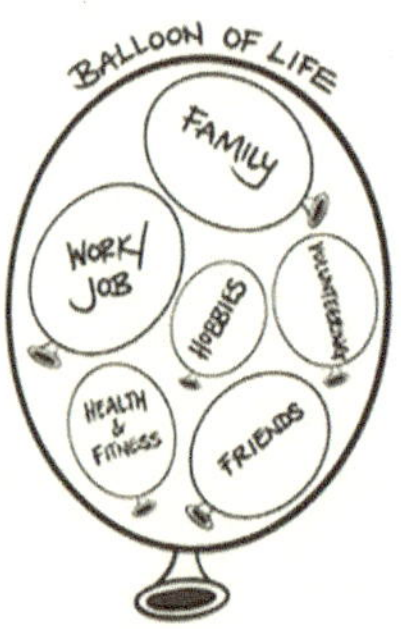

Each inner balloon can expand and contract based on the choices you make about how much time and energy you will dedicate to it. Some balloons might even have balloons within them (for example your work balloon might include your role, the projects you work on, your team, etc).

Sometimes, one balloon may need to expand because life throws a variety of wonderful and scary and heart-breaking things at you. That may mean other balloons need to deflate a little for a while. They're still there, ready and waiting for when you have the space to breathe life into them. You may find there are too many balloons, or some balloons are taking up energy you'd rather invest elsewhere.

The inner balloons are controllable or at least influenceable, based on your choices. The outer balloon is constrained by the annoying limitation of time available. You might find that the more you look after the inner balloons, the more the outer balloon feels like it's a little bit more flexible. There are some balloons that act as energy suppliers, giving back to you when you invest in them. These are joyful balloons – keep them, nourish them, love them. Get to know why these balloons give you the joy and consider how you can maximize their impact.

The space between

Almost as important as the balloons themselves is the space between them. Having 27 fully filled balloons filling every second leaves no room for anything else. If your balloons are rubbing up against each other, they're going to create that static that makes your hair stand on end. They will have you headed towards burnout quicker than you can deflate them.

We all need room to do nothing, to experience the joy of having no plans at all, maybe even to be bored for once, un-entertained, because being bored is very good for us.[2] Perhaps creating some space to be spontaneous is exactly what you need, so you can say 'Yes!' to an opportunity rather than 'I'm too busy.'

Be ready to be unashamedly selfish and protect that space. As the airlines tell us, you need to put your own oxygen mask on first. Allow your balloons the space to be friction-free, calm and moveable.

Sorting out your balloons

Here's one way to quickly size up where you want to focus some attention.

1. Identify and write down the major balloons within your life (no more than 10 for the

purposes of the exercise – pick the most important).

2. Draw them inside your balloon of life – the bigger the amount of time and energy invested, the bigger the balloon, and vice versa.
3. Give each balloon a score out of 10 (10 = consistent joy, 1 = chronic gloom). Don't overthink this – it's not a test – base it on your gut feeling.
4. Then consider:
    a. Which balloons would you like to take up more space?
    b. Which balloons would you like to take up less space?
    c. What feels out of kilter?
    d. What feels about right?
    e. What balloons are missing that should be in there?
    f. Which balloons would you like to pop?
5. Next, think about what size you'd like each balloon to be in the future, on average, and re-draw your life balloon based on this ideal.
6. In your ideal version, write in where you want your score out of 10 to be in six months' time. Be realistic!

7. Pick one inner balloon to focus on first and define one small action you can take right now.

Once you've completed this exercise, you'll have a good understanding of what's important to you, which areas are on track, which have gone off-piste and where you might want to focus your attention.

The route to WorkJoy – life

Using the active WorkJoy formula, let's see how you could use the three Es of Engagement, Energy and Experimentation within the context of *life* to cultivate WorkJoy and reframe WorkGloom.

Life	Cultivating WorkJoy	Reframing WorkGloom
Engagement	Direct your thinking towards work being a part of that bigger thing called life rather than attempting to create work/life 'balance'.	If you've got stuck with a work balloon that's squishing your other balloons out of shape (or even popping them), reframe your thinking towards what's in your control and focus there.

Life	Cultivating WorkJoy	Reframing WorkGloom
Energy	Invest your energy in defining the things that are most important in your life using the *balloons of life* activity and use this thinking to guide the choices you make.	Consider whether any balloons may need to deflate a little to create space for the things that matter most to you and remember it's ok to be selfish!
Experimentation	Experiment with giving more 'air' to a balloon that's currently bringing you joy.	Pick a balloon that is contributing to your gloom and dig deep into the who, what and why – and then do something about it!

Now that you've explored your *life* and what's important to you, in Day 4 we'll look at your *values* and how they can guide your thinking and your actions.

So what? Over to you…

1. Which balloons in your life are over- or under-inflated right now?

2. How can you create more 'space between' for rest or spontaneity?

3. Which three-E tactic will you try this week?

Day 4

Know and live your values

I know that 'values' can sound like an empty buzz word, but they are a critical piece of your WorkJoy puzzle. You'll likely find that some of the gloom you experience is when your values are not aligned to your situation. Let's start by defining what values really are.

Values, principles, behaviours

Thinking about values in an abstract way can be unhelpful. I prefer to think of them in terms of how they sit with our principles and our behaviours.

- **Values** are deeply linked to your emotions – they are *heart led*. They are the things that you care about in your life. They help you make choices and decisions that feel right for you.

- **Principles** are linked to your beliefs about what is the 'right' way to do things – they are *thought led* and influenced by your background (family, culture, environment, etc). They act as your internal moral compass.
- **Behaviours** are how you show up in the world – they are *action led*. In theory, they are the way in which you demonstrate your values and principles through what you say and what you do. When your behaviour and values are aligned, you feel good; when they're not, you can feel like you're in quick-sand and unable to find your footing.

Your values also act as an anchor point when things feel difficult, guiding you through tough times, helping you weigh up options and make choices.

Defining your personal values

There are many books and processes out there for working out what values are important to you, but here are four experiments that might help.

Opposites
• Ask yourself 'what behaviours do I dislike in others?' • Write down the opposite of those behaviours • Group the behaviours together in themes • Give each theme a word that best describes it
Free writing
• Ask yourself 'what is important to me in my life? What do I really care about?' • Set a timer for six minutes • Start writing, do not stop, do not overthink, just keep writing • Once the six minutes are completed, review your thinking and pick out the main themes • Give each theme a word that best describes it
Reverse engineering
• Ask yourself 'what behaviours do I display when I'm at my very best?' • Write a list of those behaviours • Switch them from behaviours into values words • Give each theme a word that best describes it

Crowd source
• Choose three to five people from different areas of our life who you trust and admire and who know you well • Ask them to describe you when you're at your best • Consider how their feedback relates to your behaviours • Theme the behaviours together • Give each theme a word that best describes it

Check and challenge

Once you've created a list of three to five words that describe your values, dig a little deeper and test them out.

- How do these words make you feel?
- Would you be proud if others used them to describe you?
- How often are you living them?

The link between values and purpose

Purpose is another buzzword that's often overused. Let's look at how values and purpose are linked.

Personal purpose

Finding your purpose is a quest that many people embark on, hoping it will be the magic wand that leads to a wonderful life. There's research to suggest that people who have a sense of purpose are happier (and live longer) than those that don't, but we're not necessarily talking about saving the planet here.[3] Your personal purpose does not need to be grand, bold or even particularly innovative.

The power of multi- and micro-purposes

Your purpose also doesn't have to be singular. You may have a bigger purpose to connect to and then set a daily intention. You may even have different purposes for different areas; a life-based purpose and a work-based purpose, perhaps? It could be a theme that guides how you invest your energy. This approach helps to avoid being pulled in multiple directions. It's also something that can adapt with you over the course of your life.

Your purpose can evolve over time. Some things will become more important, others less so. New things get added and others lost. Your experiences will continue to teach you what matters most, and why.

Organizational values

Many organizations talk about their values. They can reflect reality, or they can be aspirational, statements of intent. The values your organization subscribes to will inevitably have an impact on you. You may interpret what they mean through your own lens, relating them to your own thinking and experiences. Every other person in the organization will do the same thing. Whether that's ten slightly different perspectives, or 10,000 alternative views, organizational values are complex because they are not controllable.

How to find alignment with your organization

Rather than focus on the values themselves, realign your attention to the behaviours of the people around you.

- **Look to the leadership.** What behaviours do they display? What's the role model archetype around here? Do they demonstrate behaviours you can respect 70%–80% of the time?
- **Consider your colleagues.** What do your teammates and close colleagues offer in

their behaviours? Are they with you, do they support you? Have they got your back? Could you rely on them in a crisis? Do they care about you personally?

- **Delight in diversity.** A group that all has the exact same values may sound like a lovely, conflict-free place to be. In fact, it's likely to be devoid of creativity, seriously lacking in inspiration and more likely to fail than one with greater levels of cognitive diversity. Understanding and valuing different perspectives can be the key to a high-performing team. Seek out a working environment where your values are complemented by the people you are surrounded by, where the whole is greater than the sum of the parts.

The route to WorkJoy – values

Using the active WorkJoy formula, let's consider some ideas of how you could use the three Es of Engagement, Energy and Experimentation within the context of *values* to both cultivate WorkJoy and reframe WorkGloom.

Values	Cultivating WorkJoy	Reframing WorkGloom
Engagement	Explore themes or micro-purposes for your work-related projects. For example: Project A is all about collaboration, on Project B I'm dialling down my humility value so I can promote my team's work.	Direct your thinking towards how your values align with other people's. You might be surprised how just one shared approach can build a more positive relationship.
Energy	Invest your energy in defining how your personal values apply in your professional setting. Which ones are most important to you at work? How do these show up in your behaviours? (It's OK that some may be better suited to your life outside of work.)	Consider the behaviours that feel most natural and joyful to you and assess these against what you demonstrate at work. Are you missing opportunities to be yourself or is your style out of kilter?

Values	Cultivating WorkJoy	Reframing WorkGloom
Experimentation	Where can you find and lean into diversity in your work environment this week? Whose perspectives might complement rather than matching your own?	Avoid making snap judgements about what people care about by getting to know them better, especially those you find harder to connect with.

As well as directing what you do and how you do it, your values can also help you decide what you *won't* do. Get ready to think about boundaries!

So what? Over to you…

1. What are your personal values?

2. Are you able to live your values at work?

3. What values does your organization promote, and how do these align with behaviours?

Day 5
Set and strengthen your boundaries

If you get them right, boundaries can be wonderful fences that enable you to spend your time doing the work you love. Conversely, a lack of boundaries is a sure-fire way to WorkGloom! Today we'll cover the challenges of limited time and explore a model that will help you consider different types of boundaries. Let's step back first and look at how the boundaries between work and life have moved.

The blurring of boundaries

The separation between work and home life has been disappearing since the dawn of the digital era. The old structure of 9am to 5pm, at a desk in a specific location, is no longer the standard for office-based workers. Which means that, for most of us, the work day has expanded and extended. You may have found that the 'always on' culture and the post-pandemic hybrid home working approach have invaded your life.

In many ways this new flexibility is a welcome change, but the downsides can include Zoom fatigue, the loss of real, human connection and an all-pervasive, inescapable sense of overwhelm.

The issue with time

There are always just 24 hours in a day, 7 days in a week and 365 days in a year, yet many of us experience a weird relationship with time. We get lost in the flow of a project and time seems to whizz by in an instant, then we find ourselves counting the seconds until the meeting is over while time seems to slow down to a stop.

Add on extended working days and an increasingly full life together with a tendency to put off bedtime as we try to get everything done and all of this can come at the expense of sleep. Inadequate sleep can cause major physical and mental issues, let alone the impact it will have on your levels of joy. It's almost impossible to feel positive when you're tired.

Research shows that those who feel time-poor experience less joy in their life.[4] Too often the response to the question, 'how's it going?', is simply 'busy'.

You can't create more hours in the day, but you can learn how to use your time more joyfully by creating boundaries to protect your space.

The challenge with boundaries

Boundaries can make or break your mood. The challenges with creating, implementing and maintaining boundaries often fall into four categories.

1. Too strict

If your boundaries are too strict, you may fall into the trap of becoming an inflexible person who's difficult to live or work with.

2. Too flexible

If you move your boundaries at the whim of others, you risk pleasing everyone else and making your own life miserable. A boundary that isn't upheld isn't a boundary at all – you're giving everyone permission to encroach on your precious time.

3. They're someone else's, not yours

When you're on mission to change, develop or grow, you may seek out inspiration from others. Trying to copy and paste someone else's hard-earned work into your own life is likely to be a bad fit for you.

4. They're out of date

Your priorities and requirements change over time. As you evolve, so must your boundaries.

Defining your boundaries

Your boundaries will help you manage your limited time in a way that works for you. Understanding these categories of boundaries can help you decide when to stand firm and when to let things go:

- **Non-negotiables:** the boundaries you hold firmly
- **Bouncy boundaries:** the boundaries that adapt depending on the situation
- **Free-flex:** the boundaries that are the most adaptable.

Working out your boundaries

In this diagram, you'll see how the three types of boundaries work. Working from the firmly held non-negotiables, through the more nuanced bouncy boundaries that are applied based on the situation and on to the free-flex option. You can discover what your unique boundaries are by working through this experiment.

Your non-negotiable boundaries

You'll almost certainly need a few critically important, firmly held boundaries. Too many and you may become too rigid, too few and your time might be eaten by someone else.

Why: Compelling reason	Define the compelling reason for wanting to put this boundary in place. This is likely to be connected to your values.
What: The boundary I will hold firm	Define what the boundary looks like and sounds like – being as specific as possible. How will you communicate this boundary to other people?
How: Making it happen	How will you implement and maintain this boundary? What changes need to happen to make it a reality? Who needs to be involved? How will you make sure it's working?
Breaking it: The *only* times I will allow the boundary to be broken	Even with non-negotiable boundaries, there may be the exception that proves the rule. Use some situations you've found challenging before to assess the difference between a genuine exception and just flexing too far.

Your bouncy boundaries

Trying to oversimplify things can make life more difficult. There are different reasons for saying yes or no, for different situations, times and people.

Situational	Many boundaries can't be predefined as they're nuanced. You need to weigh up the pros and cons in the moment. It can be helpful to pause and understand where the situation fits into your personal priorities and values before deciding.
Conditional	This may help when you're prepared to do something for a certain person, or in a specific situation, but only if there's an acceptable quid-pro-quo. For example: 'If I do X, I'll need Y in return' or 'I can do that, but which of the other actives on my list should we deprioritize to make this happen?' or even 'I'll do it this time, but this can't happen again.'
Personal	There are some people in your life who will probably nearly always get a yes. Define who these people are up front – it will make it easier to draw the line when you need to. Who's most important? Who can make or break your day? Who always supports you? For these people, a firmly held boundary may be thrown out of the window if they need you.

Your free-flex boundaries

It's also helpful to have some situations and some people where the boundaries are much more flexible. You only need a few situations and a very limited number of people in this category. Too many and you're in danger of overcommitting and, potentially, being taken advantage of! Consider these two questions to work out where your free-flex boundaries may come into play:

What: What opportunities would you make your best efforts to say *yes* to whenever it's possible to do so?

For example:

- **Work-related:** a career-enhancing opportunity, the chance to learn something new, a conversation with an interesting person
- **Life-related:** having fun doing something that is pure joy (hobbies, sports, going out for dinner – whatever floats your joy boat)

Who: Who are the people you would move mountains for?

For example:

- **Work-related:** a brilliant boss/mentor dedicated to developing your career always gets a yes (as opposed to a terrible boss who takes advantage needing stronger boundaries!)
- **Life-related:** key people for whom you are there, whatever they need of you and whenever they need you

Implementing boundaries

Once you know what you want your boundaries to look like, the next challenge is to implement them. This means making choices on what you will invest your time into and who you will spend it with. In many situations, the answer may be obvious, you'll have that gut feel that says a big *yes* or a definite *no*. When you're not sure, trying out these three stages may help you work through each situation:

1. **Pause.** The first step to implementing better boundaries is to simply pause while you mentally tot up the score. To avoid offence, try phrases such as 'What an offer! Can I get back to you tomorrow with an answer?' or 'I'm really honoured you thought of me... let me check if I can fully commit as I would want to be all in on this one.'
2. **Ponder.** Considering how your options fit with your boundaries and what each might mean. If you say yes, what might you gain from the experience? What might you need to drop to allow the space for it? And if you say no, what might you miss out on? What might you be able to say yes to instead? It might help to get some outside perspective.

3. **Pick.** Your final choice may not be as binary as yes or no. It could be yes with caveats, or yes but not now. It could be not just yet.

Saying *no*

Saying no can feel hard, it's why so many people find themselves overcommitted. You want to please people, you don't want to let them down, fear of missing out (FOMO)... But it's possible to get better at this.

Saying *no* when you want to say *no*

The trick with a well-delivered *no* is to be clear and concise. No need to apologize and make excuses. Try:

- 'It's going to be a *no* from me as I'm focusing on other priorities right now.'
- 'Thank you for the kind offer, it's not something I can commit to right now.'
- 'Although I'm grateful for the offer, this one's not where my passion lies.'

Saying *no* when you want to say *yes*

You've worked through the steps and made your decision, but you might want to leave the door open for the future:

- 'I would love to, yet I simply don't have the time.'
- 'If there's another opportunity in the future, I would love to say yes then.'

You could even use this as an opportunity to advocate for another person:

- 'Have you thought about asking X – they're brilliant at this?'

Saying *yes* when you want to say *no*

Perhaps your boss has asked you to complete a task and saying *no* may be a career-limiting move. Maybe there's something you're doing because it's for a person you care about. Understand that you've made the choice to say yes then participate fully (without moaning) and see if you can eke out a little joy in the process.

The route to WorkJoy – boundaries

Using the active WorkJoy formula, let's explore some ideas of how you could use the three Es of Engagement, Energy and Experimentation within the context of *boundaries* to both cultivate WorkJoy and reframe WorkGloom.

Boundaries	Cultivating WorkJoy	Reframing WorkGloom
Engagement	Direct your thinking towards the what (situation) and the who (people) when you're setting boundaries rather than towards the boundaries themselves – this will make them more realistic and easier to implement.	Remember that there will always be times when the boundaries go out the window – that's real life. Don't give up because it didn't work one time.
Energy	Invest your energy in defining your non-negotiable, bouncy and free-flex boundaries to allow different levels of adaptability in real life.	Rather than rushing to an answer and regretting your decision, invest a little time in pausing and pondering before you pick.

Boundaries	Cultivating WorkJoy	Reframing WorkGloom
Experimentation	Share your boundaries with your colleagues, as it's much easier for people to respect boundaries when they are clear (e.g. 'I prefer 50-minute meetings to make sure I'm fully engaged and not rushing to my next one').	Experiment with saying *no* in clear and concise ways instead of creating elaborate excuses!

So what? Over to you…

1. Where have your work and life boundaries blurred most?

2. Which non-negotiable boundary will you set or reinforce this week?

3. How could you make one 'bouncy' boundary more resilient?

Day 6
Rewrite your work story

Stories are at the heart of how humans communicate. When a story exists only in your mind, it's easy for it to get bent out of shape and chip away at your self-belief. Today, we'll explore how to take control of your narrative.

Your story world

You've experienced stories all your life, from childhood bedtime to 'show and tell' at school to key moments like sharing your story at job interviews.

You interact with the stories in your head and the stories of others, a vast web of information and connection. The stories in your head have an enormous impact on how you view things and how you feel. Let's dig into some of the core stories and explore how you can create a more joyful approach.

The stories you tell yourself about yourself

Depending on the type of stories you tell yourself, they can be the bedrock on which to build real joy or the influencer of gloom. Without any light to shine perspective on them, with no one to listen to them or challenge them, they can cause all kinds of problems, including *imposter syndrome* and *unchecked arrogance*:

- **Imposter syndrome** is that feeling you have when you don't feel good enough, worthy enough or when you feel like you don't know enough and someone is about to expose your lack of expertise. It's a horrible, exhausting feeling that can influence both how you think about yourself and how you behave.
- **Unchecked arrogance** sits at the other end of this see-saw. Arrogance is thinking (and acting like) you are more important, know more or are better than other people, and it's often caused by a lack of self-awareness.

There's a difference between confidence and arrogance, and there's also a difference between humility and imposter syndrome.

The antidote to both ends of this continuum is the middle ground of *self-belief* – trust in yourself. You know your strengths and you know you can take action to improve. Building self-belief can be tricky, especially if you have been underestimating or undervaluing yourself and your abilities for some time, but working on it can be transformational to your levels of WorkJoy. Start by noticing your successes, however small, and by surrounding yourself with people who encourage and support you.

The stories you tell other people about yourself

A strong foundation for WorkJoy is having clarity on what your story is and being able to share it with others, no matter how uncomfortable that feels. It doesn't matter if you feel your own story is boring or inconsequential – stories are meant to be told and yours will be interesting and valuable to others. Having stories ready to tell can be useful to:

- Remind yourself of who you are, your journey, your successes, the hurdles you have jumped over, the ways you've grown and where you're heading to.
- Easily recall and share when someone asks you a question about yourself (a pre-prepared,

ready-to-go, engaging version rather than the put-on-the-spot version).

- Act as the foundation of a conversation about you, your background, your career, where you want to head (helping people to understand how they can help you).

Here are four core personal stories to build, rehearse and share.

Story	Basic structure
My potted history: How I became who I am today	• **Act one:** The Past (where I've come from and who I was) • **Act two:** The Present (where I am now and who I am) • **Act three:** The Future (where I'm heading to and who I want to be)
One minute on me: The elevator pitch	• What I do and why I do it • What opportunities I'm after
Future fantasy: Where I'm heading	• What I want the future to look/sound/feel like • How I plan to get there • What support I need to make it happen

Story	Basic structure
Deep dive: Aka Me 101	• More life-related stuff • My values and beliefs • Where my strengths are and what I've learned • What I'm working on

Once you've written a story, you need to say it *out loud*. Your brain connects differently to context when it hears you saying it than it does when you read it. So, get practising!

The stories you tell yourself about other people

You hold an infinite number of stories in your head about other people; from those you put on pedestals to those for whom you have disdain. Confirmation bias seeks out and logs the evidence either way. At their best, the stories we tell ourselves about those we put on pedestals motivate us to act. At their worst, they create a sense of competition; comparititus is one of the most relentless joy thieves in the world. For those we designate villains, each move they make reinforces our belief that they are simply no good.

The truth is, of course, that all humans are wonderfully flawed. Putting someone on a pedestal of perfection doesn't help you (or them). It doesn't allow for real-life ups and downs, for mistakes, for getting it wrong. Likewise, assuming that someone is all bad because they've done or said something you don't like is creating a story that doesn't help build a better relationship.

'I didn't get promoted because my boss is a terrible person' is a much easier tale to spin than the complex reality.

What you experience of others is just the tip of the iceberg. Underneath the water line is a human being with challenges, struggles and successes. Assuming that people are doing the best they can is usually a good way to go.

The stories other people tell other people about you

Being too concerned with what other people say about you can make you try to change in an inauthentic way, moulding yourself in someone else's vision, losing parts of the real you. But care too little and you risk never growing. Taking time to create and share the stories you want people to tell about you can help to mitigate this challenge.

The route to WorkJoy – stories

Using the active WorkJoy formula, let's explore some ideas of how you could use the three Es of Engagement, Energy and Experimentation within the context of *stories* to both cultivate WorkJoy and reframe WorkGloom.

Stories	Cultivating WorkJoy	Reframing WorkGloom
Engagement	Remember that there are multiple stories going on at any one time and you are not in control of all of them, yet you can influence many of them (especially the ones in your head!).	Avoid casting people as victors or villains; instead, engage your empathy and respect that everyone has things going on in their life that you don't know about.
Energy	Invest your energy in nurturing your *self-belief* by getting a story out of your head and saying it out loud, with enthusiasm!	Step away from conversations that disrespect other people and invest your energy into actively advocating for your colleagues.

Stories	Cultivating WorkJoy	Reframing WorkGloom
Experimentation	Create a personal story and start sharing it with different people and see how they respond. Then refine and keep building the stories you share.	Keep a log of praise you receive and refer to it often. This will realign your focus, remind you of your strengths and balance out some of the negative stories you may tell yourself.

So what? Over to you…

1. What stories do you tell yourself? How helpful are they?

2. How would you rate your current level of self-belief?

3. What story would you like others to tell about you?

Day 7
Build a joyful squad

If you're going to love your job, you need people around you who can provide you with high levels of support and great challenge to keep you growing – these people are your squaddies. It isn't about who likes you or who your work friends are. Better labels might be professional partners, active allies or constructive colleagues. Today we're going to look at how to build and maintain a truly powerful squad.

Squad positions

Let's look at your role before moving on to explore six key squad roles. You're the headliner, with hiring and firing rights. You'll need to engage your squad and be ready to lead them, being clear about what you need. Remember, this isn't a one-way street. Ask yourself, 'What can I offer to my squaddies? What position could I hold in their squad?' If they don't need you right now, why not pay it forward and offer your squad services to someone who could use your unique blend of skills? There's real joy to be found in giving and the more you give, the more you'll get – the joy of reciprocity![5]

Now let's look in turn at the other roles in your squad...

Cheerleaders:

- always see the good in you, focusing their attention on your strengths

- build you up and openly talk about what you do well
- will give you a pep talk or a self-belief boost when you need it
- don't have to be 'in it' with you; they can stand apart from your work.

Challengers:

- give you the feedback and advice you need to grow, learn and change
- look you in the eye and give you the home truths
- hold you accountable for making progress
- are your point of call when you need no-holds-barred guidance.

Comrades:

- are in it with you, right by your side, experiencing the same things as you
- offer unwavering commitment to you through good times and bad
- are always there for you whatever you need
- are your first call when you succeed and when you have a crisis.

Creatives:

- help you spark ideas, consider alternative options and define solutions
- offer questions to get your brain engaged
- share their insight from a different viewpoint, expanding your thinking
- are the people whom you call when you're stuck in a rut or in a set way of thinking.

Connectors:

- locate the people you need and introduce you to them
- have a radar for who could help, support and guide you
- generously use their vast personal network to enhance your network
- are the people you go to with the question 'who can help with...?'

Conjurers:

- create the magic that makes you feel optimistic, determined and brave
- have an indescribable quality that emanates a combination of warmth and strength
- provide you with the tools to do what you need, even when it's hard

- appear and disappear in a puff of smoke when they have worked their magic.

You might find that some people take on more than one role, or that roles shift over time. What matters is that your squad covers a healthy balance of support, challenge and inspiration.

Squad membership

A great squad can flex. Some members will be 'lifers', central characters in the story of your working life; others will be 'reason and/or season' squaddies, supporting a transition or helping you gain an essential skill, then leaving your squad when the time is right.

Take care to 'right size' your squad depending on your situation. Too big a squad is unwieldy, and you won't be able to pay as much attention to everyone. Too small and you might end up asking too much of some people or needing a different skill set. It's a fine balance of small enough to develop and maintain relationships of trust and care (which take investment) and big enough to fulfil the roles you need. The more you work with your squad, the more experience you'll have of finding the right combinations of people for the right moments in time.

It's worth doing a regular squaddie audit. Are the roles still appropriate? Is there a gap? Do you need to say au revoir to squaddies because things have changed?

Building your squad

If you spot a gap or need a boost of different energy, it's time to actively search out and recruit some new members for your squad. Here's how:

1. Pick a role you would like to strengthen in your squad and define the skills you are looking for.
2. Identify some people in your network who might fit the bill.
3. Book in time to meet with them and talk.

Asking for help can feel awkward, but the worst that can happen is that someone says no. Rejection may feel awful, but it is usually short-lived. Regret for not doing something often lasts a lot longer and can eat away at your self-belief.

It's unlikely that someone you have a limited relationship with right now will go straight to being a core squaddie. Start by asking them for their help in something *small*, something *specific* and something *simple* for them to do.

Try this three-step process:

1. Share the context and where you see their strengths (share your feedback).
2. State the challenge you need help with (declare your goal).
3. Ask for what you need (remembering to keep it small, specific and simple).

For example: You want to build your challengers and are keen to be better at speaking up in meetings. You've identified someone who you admire for doing this well. When you meet with them, you might say something like this:

1. I really admire how you always speak up in our meetings. The way you structure your thoughts and share them in such a concise way is where I want to get to.
2. I often leave meetings wishing I'd said something, and I've made a commitment to say at least one thing in each meeting going forward.
3. Would you be able to share with me how you structure and share your thoughts while in the room?

Nurturing your squad

Once you've built your squad, nurture those relationships. Set up a time to meet or talk with each squaddie – a virtual coffee is fine. Then share directly with them how they have helped you and the impact they have had. Try this three-step method to structure your feedback:

1. Thank them for what they give you – be specific.
2. Share how it made you feel.
3. Describe the impact their support has on you.

The route to WorkJoy – squads

Using the active WorkJoy formula, let's explore some ideas of how you could use the three Es of Engagement, Energy and Experimentation within the context of *squads* to both cultivate WorkJoy and reframe WorkGloom.

Squads	Cultivating WorkJoy	Reframing WorkGloom
Engagement	Consider what roles you are playing in other people's squads and proactively offer to help (e.g. ask, 'what can I do to help you with X, Y, Z?').	Check in with yourself to see whether you're being a good squaddie for others: if not, do something to change.
Energy	Spend time understanding who's in your squad now and where you have some gaps to fill (e.g. I'm great for cheerleaders but need some more challengers).	Invest your energy with the right people, in the right places and on the right subjects.
Experimentation	Try out asking someone to help you with a challenge you're having or a goal you want to achieve. Remember to work with something *small*, *specific* and *simple*.	Remember to share your gratitude to those who help you, sharing your feedback and letting them know the impact they have had (and feel the joy of reciprocity).

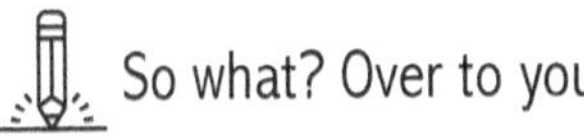

1. Who are the core members of your current joyful squad?

2. Which roles are well-represented, and which are missing?

3. What's one thing you could do this week to strengthen a squad connection?

Day 8

Shift your career perspective

There's no one magic career formula. But there are many ways to make your moves more joyful.

Different types of career moves

These days careers are rarely linear. You can have multiple roles with different organizations – either over time or at the same time. If you have a passion you want to pursue, you can create a side-hustle. There is a whole world of opportunity, ready for you to build your own path to a destination you love.

Let's look at what different types of career moves are possible. These seven examples are possible in many organizations and you'll probably recognize some you've already made. They can stand alone, and some can be combined. It's not an exhaustive list, but it's a good starting point to consider which options might be right for you.

Selectively sideways

These moves are some of the most valuable moves you can make. Often taken up within the same subject matter, area of expertise or profession, these sideways(ish) moves enable you to build your knowledge, skills and breadth of experience. They allow for gradual development over time and can expand your horizons by exposing you to different people, skills and challenges. They help you build a wider network and institutional knowledge and allow you to collaborate more effectively. All of which is career gold dust.

This move can also set you up for adventures outside your current organization, expanding your horizons with different people, products or services.

It might allow you to develop into a new specialism or industry, having developed new knowledge and skills. You may even discover a gap in the market and set up your own thing to fill that gap.

Tactical trip

In a tactical trip, you apply your skills in a new context, broadening your experience, deepening your understanding and opening up new opportunities. This could mean moving between a specialist function and a customer function or moving from a corporate to a cool new start-up. Tactical trips are some of the most common of career moves, especially for those with a transferable set of skills.

If your skills are in demand, you may also be able to secure a role with increased salary/benefits (it's often easier to gain a pay rise through a tactical trip than it is to do so by growing within your existing role).

Long haul ladder

Most often found in organizations with more traditional, hierarchical structures, a ladder move involves applying for and/or being promoted into a new role at a more senior level, either within your current workplace or as part of a move to a new organization.

A ladder move often relies on there being a vacancy to fill, so you might feel stuck if you're in a niche area or a smaller organization. Perhaps you're ready to take on your boss's job, but they're showing no sign of moving? Or maybe the next role you want requires management experience, which you don't have (yet), and you can't get it until you get a job that requires it... there are missing rungs thwarting your ascent.

You can craft ladder moves yourself – perhaps you've noticed a role that's really needed in your team? Or maybe there's a project role or secondment that could act as a temporary rung on your ladder, getting you the experience you require to turn it from a stop gap to a solid step?

Executive escalator

In some industries, the clear pathway from junior team member to executive leader is part of the organizational structure. In law, accountancy, some medical careers and academia, time- and skills-based progression are still the norm. In these cases, the routes are planned for you. You're likely to have to put in the hours in both learning and delivering results at each level. You may have to pitch yourself, present your story and prove that you are worthy of the next promotion, with each stage becoming more challenging.

A word of caution – executive escalators and long-haul ladders

Hierarchical structures are built as pyramids, and at the pinnacle is a very small set of leaders. As you ascend there is usually a combination of increasing responsibilities and demands placed on you. Additional hours become the norm and expectations change. They may come with the lure of more money, benefits and status, but also with the requirement to manage and lead people, which you might or might not love.

These career moves hook you in and keep you firmly on a predefined path. If you're in one of these careers, take a moment occasionally to check in with yourself. Is the outcome still what you really want?

Deep dive

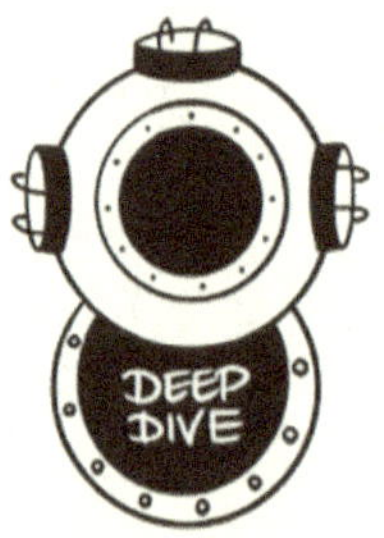

There are some roles and industries where being a specialist on a specific subject is highly valued. It's likely that your work will be at the core of the business and people will rely heavily on you to apply your expertise effectively and efficiently. Many deep divers find themselves gainfully employed in this way throughout their careers; others might lack a sense of career growth.

Make sure you keep your eyes on the horizon, as disruption can quickly make highly valued skills redundant. So, keep an eye out, keep learning, and re-specialize yourself before the market forces you to!

Active adventure

The active adventure lets you step out of your current role, specialism or profession and into discovering new things, working with different people in new environments – a fresh challenge. You'll need to learn new skills, develop your strengths and be ready to throw yourself in at the deep end.

Some may say they are riskier moves, as you risk being seen as a Jack/Jackie of all trades, but in many places, breadth and diversity of experience is becoming highly valued.

Structured adventures may come in the form of graduate or management development programmes early on in your career. They can also be in the form of secondments, cover roles or fixed term opportunities. Or you can step out of employment into entrepreneurship. There are almost unlimited opportunities if you're prepared to pack your rucksack and head out on an adventure – the world really is your oyster.

Grounded growth

Having a great career is not all about hopping about between roles or organizations: some people, especially those who value deep relationships, prefer grounded growth. This isn't a stop and stick; it requires commitment to staying up to date, developing skills and expertise – feeding your roots and allowing yourself to expand into the organizational space.

To make this (un)move work well, you'll need to feel really connected to your role and your organization. Your value to the business will expand as your institutional understanding increases over time and people will be lost without you (although it's important to remember that, often, no role is indispensable). There is huge value to having grounded people in organizations and much joy to be had within these roles. You don't always have to be chasing the next big thing.

The route to WorkJoy – careers

Using the active WorkJoy formula, let's explore some ideas of how you could use the three Es of Engagement, Energy and Experimentation within the context of *careers* to both cultivate WorkJoy and reframe WorkGloom.

Careers	Cultivating WorkJoy	Reframing WorkGloom
Engagement	Define what types of moves you've made in the past to anchor yourself in your career story so far and see how it might inform your future.	Consider how any potential career move will fit into your life – and do the maths before you make a move. The grass isn't always greener on the other side.

Careers	Cultivating WorkJoy	Reframing WorkGloom
Energy	Point your energy towards the shape of your possible career moves, rather than specific roles. This can broaden your thinking and open unexplored opportunities (e.g. exploring grounded growth in addition to the deep dive).	If your current remuneration is getting you gloomy, try exploring what your role offers you beyond financial reward (e.g. does it give you flexibility? Are you learning? Do you have a great boss?).
Experimentation	Experiment with DIY-ing your own career pathway. Seek out potential roles and talk to people about what you're looking for – they may know of just the thing.	Invest in doing your current job well, engage (or re-engage) with it, and experiment with reconnecting to the joy you once had. Even if you know you're going to move on, this will help you transition positively into your next role.

So what? Over to you…

1. Which type(s) of career moves have you taken so far?

2. What did they give you?

3. What might you be considering for your next move?

Day 9
Tame the gloom

Organizations come in many shapes and sizes, but there are many common features that build joy or have us grappling with gloom irrespective of their purpose, style or sector. Do you recognize any of these?

Sources of WorkGloom

Life takeover

Your whole life belongs to the organization. From getting up earlier to fit in emails before you get stuck in meetings that only add to your to-do list, to trying to make a global call work between time zones in the evening, your brain gets filled with the never-ending list of priorities that squeeze your other priorities to the edges.

Change

Everyone wants something in their organization to change. Yet when things do change, it can be hard to handle. Enforced change takes away choices and can leave you feeling disempowered. Maybe the change is too small or the wrong solution, so you get disappointed. Or it's too big and you feel a loss of control. Change is inevitable but approaching it with a WorkJoy mindset helps. Even restructuring and redundancies can be reframed as redirection!

Wrong-sized jobs

Managers are notoriously bad at defining the right size and shape of jobs. A role advertised as a standard 37 hours a week may take only 20 hours, or, more likely, 55! Usually this is not deliberate – it's a hard thing to estimate – but where organizations get it wrong is doubling down on their guesswork and insisting a job can be done within a certain time frame when all the evidence points in the other direction.

If you find yourself in this position, it's time to have a conversation with your boss and work out what's realistic and what the route to making it 'right sized' is. You may also want to review your boundaries (see Day 5!).

Scope creep

This one can be a source of WorkJoy or WorkGloom depending on which way the creep is directed! Often, job descriptions are written based on what the previous incumbent did, or if it's a new role, it's a wish list formed in the imagination of the creator. Even if you manage to start on script, it's highly likely you won't stay there. This may mean stepping out of your comfort zone – learning different parts of the business, expanding your skill set and broadening your horizons and potential career opportunities. That can be brilliant, but sometimes it can move you backwards. That might be acceptable in the short term, but if it's all of this, all the time, consider whether the evolved role is what you really want.

Fake promotions

When promotions involve job title changes and reward, they're real. But sometimes organizations use fake promotions: someone leaves and you take on their workload for no additional reward. Or there's a big project and your boss says, 'this will be great for your profile in the organization'. You take on the challenge of the project, you work your socks off, then suddenly it's become business as usual. Being open to development can be a source of WorkJoy: the key is to know when an opportunity is genuine, understand where and how it will enable your development and be clear about what the expectations are. Again, it's an open conversation to have with your boss. Tread carefully, as you don't want the opportunity to disappear.

Imbalanced loyalty

Consider what sacrifices you make on the organization's behalf – unpaid overtime, the giving of yourself, your knowledge and your skills, the times you chose to stay when you could have left. If restructuring was on the cards, would your organization offer you the same loyalty? The point here isn't about having no loyalty, it's remembering that an organization isn't a person – you're married to the equivalent of a robot, not a human.

Have enough loyalty: not too much and not too little. Engage yourself with your work, get involved in your organization. Don't sacrifice too much of you, or your life, for it. There's no such thing as a job for life.

Square peg – round hole

You have a human need to belong, to be valued and respected for being yourself, not just for the work you do. Sometimes it feels right; sometimes you feel like a square peg in a round hole. You may try to adjust yourself to fit in, shaving the edges, squishing into uncomfortable spaces, attempting to change who you are. This rarely leads to joy.

A feeling of lack of belonging can stem from different reasons, including being somehow different, from demographic factors like race, gender and disability to style factors like levels of introversion and extroversion and levels of creativity. If you're not respected for the difference you bring but excluded because of it, that's toxic (and unlikely to change).

Is this organization right for you?

How do you know whether to stay in an organization and when to leave? The answer is nearly always 'it depends'. You'll never know in advance if the choice you make is the 'right' one. You can only go on the information you have at the time. Let both facts and feelings guide you:

- Facts offer perspective and help you navigate your path
- Feelings allow you to connect with, understand and seek out the joy, whether you stay or go.

Love the one you're with

Your level of love for your organization can range from the throes of passion to the 'I know you by heart' phase to 'better the devil you know' and even 'I wish I never have to see you again!' And it can be complicated: you could be feeling wonderful about your team yet feeling unconnected with this work itself. Perhaps you're ready to break up with the organization yet you're loving your customers. Maybe your organization does inspirational work that you love, yet the team isn't quite your cup of tea.

Whether it's a small niggle or you're heading towards a separation, it can help to remind yourself why you decided to hook up with this job in the first place. There must have been a reason you wanted to work at this organization. Have you lost sight of that connection? Does that reason no longer serve you as it once did?

Falling back in love

Here are three experiments you can try out to seek out reconnection with your organization:

1. **Go on a first date.** Sometimes you're just a bit bored and not seeing the great things your organization has to offer. Try diving deeper into your projects, getting to know your team better. You'll almost certainly find something new and exciting that will rekindle your WorkJoy.
2. **Put on your rose-tinted spectacles.** Consciously spend some time focusing on the good stuff and working out where the joy comes from.
3. **Go on a work safari.** Explore beyond your current role, team and context, finding guides from different areas and seeking out feedback from the locals. What do you discover?

There is no such thing as a 'perfect' organization, so whether you decide to stay or go the key is understanding the reasons why you are actively making that choice. Exploring whether you can fall (back) in love with your organization before you start divorce proceedings will stand you in good stead. Even if the answer is still 'get me out of here!', you'll be doing it from a better-informed place of perspective rather than running for the hills. It can also help you have a joyful exit.

Joyful goodbye

If you decide to leave an organization, always aim to do so on good terms and avoid burning any bridges. You may want to boomerang back one day, and the people you've worked with in the past are often those that offer or connect you to a future career move. At the very least be professional but ideally aim to leave as an advocate. Send gratitude emails to those who have supported you and shout about what a great time you've had to your replacement, maybe recommend the organization as a great place to work on LinkedIn or Glassdoor.

Leaving with bad feelings and a stroppy rant, especially if done publicly or identifiably, can harm your future prospects. That bitterness, even if it was caused by an organization that didn't do its best for you, is in no way attractive to a future employer. It will put them off hiring you and if you carry that bad feeling with you, it will taint any interviews or probation periods. You will get labelled as miserable – full of gloom. People are attracted to joy, so choose your attitude carefully.

The route to WorkJoy – organizations

Using the active WorkJoy formula, let's explore some ideas of how you could use the three Es of Engagement, Energy and Experimentation within the context of *organizations* to both cultivate WorkJoy and reframe WorkGloom.

Organizations	Cultivating WorkJoy	Reframing WorkGloom
Engagement	Notice all the different ways your organization brings you joy, so you know where to focus your attention.	Remember that most people within the organizations you work for are trying their best and that there is no such thing as the perfect organization.

Organizations	Cultivating WorkJoy	Reframing WorkGloom
Energy	Invest your energy in seeking out more of the things about the organization that bring you joy (e.g. if it's about the people, join a networking group, or if it's about the customers, get more connected with their needs).	Reframe the choices you are making about where you invest your energy (e.g. if it's not the right organization for you, invest in finding the right place for you rather than being gloomy about where you are right now).
Experimentation	Experiment with developing solutions to the organizational issues you observe (e.g. getting involved in employee focus groups or volunteering to be part of improvement project teams).	Try out the first dates, work safari, and rose-tinted spectacles experiments to reconnect with your organization (and discover hidden opportunities for joy!).

So what? Over to you...

1. What stage is your relationship with your organization at?

2. How might you go about falling back in love with your job?

3. How might you deal with the negative aspects?

Day 10
Make joy a habit

Loving your job isn't a one-off project; it's something you build into your everyday work life. Today we're going to focus on how to sustain your WorkJoy over the long haul, and that comes down to the habits you choose.

Habits

Habits are the brain's autopilot: they make for efficient responses to most situations. Unfortunately, not all habits are helpful, and some are damaging. Harnessing helpful habits – and unhooking from unhelpful ones – will transform your experience at work. Some examples to get you started:

Helpful habits
• Going for a daily walk • Asking questions to get clarity • Investing in your squad • Learning something new every day • Reflecting on your day • Keeping a log of successes • Drinking water
Unhelpful habits
• Stewing on past conversations • Working late • Worrying about the unknown • Binge watching TV • Procrastinating • Scrolling social media • Forgetting to fuel yourself

Building helpful habits

Try these four different ways of building a new habit.

Reduce the friction

Find ways to make new habits easier to do. For example:

- To build the habit of speaking up more in meetings, you could write down some questions before a meeting starts so that you don't have to create them on the spot
- To build the habit of going to the gym before starting work, you could put your sports clothes out the night before.

Temptation bundling

Couple the instantly gratifying 'want to' activities with the 'need to' behaviour providing long-term benefits. For example:

- To build the habit of focusing on getting the hard thing done, focus your attention on it while listening to your favourite playlist
- To build a habit of eating healthily, allow yourself a Netflix binge combined with eating a healthy snack.

Habit stacking

Utilize the helpful habits you already have by coupling them with the new thing you want to do. For example:

- To build the habit of planning your day, you could stack it onto your morning coffee/tea routine
- To build the habit of mindfulness in the morning, you could stack it onto brushing your teeth.

Habit directed

Move from being goal directed to being habit directed. For example:

- Instead of 'I want to build my knowledge of leadership', try, 'I'll read a book/watch a TED talk for 30 minutes at 7pm every Wednesday.'
- Instead of 'I want to get fit, so I'll go to the gym', try, 'when I wake up at 6.30am on Tuesdays and Thursdays, I'll go to the gym.'

Experiment with some of these habit hacks and see how they work for you.

Disrupting unhelpful habits

If hacking your habits helps to build helpful ones, what can you do with the unhelpful habits that seem to be hardwired? Here's a process to help you work out why they're there and what to do about them!

The NECTAR method

Notice – when does your unhelpful habit happen, and how does it show up? What's your reaction?

Evaluate – work out why this habit came about – did it once serve a purpose? What's its impact now, and potentially in the future?

Consider – how has it impacted your story so far? How might your story change without it?

Tactics – how might you disrupt/replace this habit? Ask your squad for suggestions!

Adapt – start adapting to a new way of thinking and acting. Don't expect perfection, but recognize progress.

Repeat - Repeat, adapt, repeat until rewiring is complete.

1. Which helpful habit could you start tomorrow that would boost your joy?

2. Which habit hack will you use to help build it?

3. Which unhelpful habit is stealing your joy – and how could you disrupt it?

Conclusion

By now you've learned that loving your job is ultimately up to you. You can choose to create and cultivate joy in your working life; you don't have to wait for someone else to create it for you. You can't fail because you're not aiming for perfection, you're aiming for progress. Every step you take will either move you towards more joy or give you a valuable lesson in what doesn't work for you. Give yourself permission to embark on this adventure.

What will you do next?

It's time to set yourself an intention to create more joy. Make it small, make it something you can start work on right now. Here are a few reminders:

- Focus your attention on the good stuff
- Reset your expectations for reality, not perfection
- Direct your energy towards action and experimentation

- Create boundaries that allow you to spend time on what's important in your life
- Identify the potential joy in any situation
- Consciously re-craft the stories you tell yourself
- Actively craft your own career path
- Evolve your thinking and actions by taking incremental action to build habits that help and let go of habits that hinder.

You don't have to wait for the perfect moment, the perfect role or the perfect organization – they may never come.

Start where you are. Pick one idea and try it. Notice what happens. Build on it. And share your joy with others – because joy is contagious.

Endnotes

[1] A. Liu, 'Making joy a priority at work' in *Harvard Business Review* (17 July 2019). Available from: https://hbr.org/2019/07/making-joy-a-priority-at-work [accessed 9 August 2025].

[2] S. Heshmat, '5 benefits of boredom' in *Psychology Today* (4 April 2020). Available from: www.psychologytoday.com/gb/blog/science-choice/202004/5-benefits-boredom [accessed 12 August 2025].

[3] M.J. Barkan, 'Why it's important to find your purpose in life (with 3 helpful tips)' in *Tracking Happiness* (3 July 2022). Available from: www.trackinghappiness.com/important-to-have-purpose-in-life/ [accessed 12 August 2025].

[4] A. Whillans, 'Time for happiness' in *Harvard Business Review* (24 January 2019). Available from: https://hbr.org/2019/01/time-for-happiness [accessed 12 August 2025].

[5] A. Grant, *Give and Take: Why Helping Others Drives Our Success* (2014).

Enjoyed this?
Then you'll love...

WorkJoy by Beth Stallwood

Business Book Awards 2024 Finalist: Highly Commended

The People's Book Prize 2023/24 Shortlisted Title

Dreading Monday? Feeling stuck in your career? Frustrated with your boss?

Here's the ouchy (but awesome) bit: The only person who can fix it is you.

Beth Stallwood is a sought-after coach, facilitator, speaker and consultant, specializing in helping people find more joy at work and helping organizations nurture their people. She's distilled years of experience into the practical WorkJoy toolkit, inspiring you to take ownership of your working life by:

- Breaking free from 'work/life balance' and un-blurring your boundaries

- Reframing relationships with your organization, boss and support squad
- Letting go of limiting beliefs and crafting big goals that won't go in the bin.

You'll spend more than a third of your lifetime working, so there's no better time to take the wheel and start creating more WorkJoy than right now.

Other *6-Minute Smarts* titles

Beating Burnout (based on *The Burnout Bible* by Rachel Philpotts)

Building Great Teams (based on *Workshop Culture* by Alison Coward)

Collaborate Better (based on *Collabor(h)ate* by Deb Mashek PhD)

Customer Success Essentials (based on *The Customer Success Pioneer* by Kellie Lucas)

Do Change Better (based on *How to be a Change Superhero* by Lucinda Carney)

Find Your Confidence (based on *Coach Yourself Confident* by Julie Smith)

Find Your Purpose (based on *The Purpose Handbook* by Eloise Skinner)

Get That Promotion (based on *Getting On* by Joanna Gaudoin)

Grow Your Product Business (based on *Tame Your Tiger* by Catherine Erdly)

How to be Happy at Work (based on *My Job Isn't Working!* by Michael Brown)

How to Get to Know Your Customer (based on *Do Penguins Eat Peaches?* by Katie Tucker)

The Inclusion Mindset (based on *Beyond Discomfort* by Nadia Nagamootoo)

The Listening Leader (based on *The Listening Shift* by Janie Van Hool)

Managing Big Teams (based on *Big Teams* by Tony Llewellyn)

Mastering People Management (based on *Mission: To Manage* by Marianne Page)

No-Fluff Soft Skills (based on *Soft Skills, Hard Results* by Anne Taylor)

No Nonsense PR (based on *Hype Yourself* by Lucy Werner)

Present Like a Pro (based on *Executive Presentations* by Jacqui Harper)

Reimagine Your Career (based on *Work/ Life Flywheel* by Ollie Henderson)

Sales Made Simple (based on *More Sales Please* by Sara Nasser Dalrymple)

The Speed Storytelling Toolkit (based on *Exposure* by Felicity Cowie)

Stay Focused (based on *Attention!* by Rob Hatch)

Write to Think (based on *Exploratory Writing* by Alison Jones)

Look out for more titles coming soon! Visit www.practicalinspiration.com for all our latest titles.

www.ingramcontent.com/pod-product-compliance
Lightning Source LLC
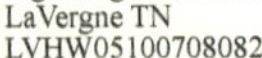
LaVergne TN
LVHW051007080826
845145LV00009B/2496

9781788608985